A Quick Crib to

TELEVISION STAGE MANAGEMENT

by Stephen Dinsdale

in association with

Christopher Sandeman & Susan Hedden

BBC Television Training

First published in 1994
BBC Television Training
BBC Elstree Centre
Clarendon Road
Borehamwood
Hertfordshire

Throughout this book the pronoun
'he' should also be taken to refer to 'she'
and vice versa. Similarly read 'woman' and
'man' and vice versa.

General Editor: Gordon Croton
Design and production: Shirley Greenfield
Illustrations: Nick Skelton

Printed by Able Printing Ltd
Paddock Wood
Kent
England

Contents

Specimen Paperwork

INTRODUCTION

The job of stage manager in television and film is so varied and all-encompassing that it would be impossible to cover all aspects of it in detail. The job varies from show to show. What we attempt to do here is to cover most aspects as helpfully as possible without going into pointless detail which will vary from company to company and situation to situation. The BBC will do some things differently to a small independent company with a staff of three and a cat — but in both situations some broad 'rules' usually apply. Those are what we are concerned with here.

Stage management is covered by various titles in the television and film industries so that things can sometimes be a little confusing.

A question of identity

In **film**, the director is assisted by the production manager (who usually stays in the office and handles the administration) and the first assistant director who is responsible for the day-to-day running of the shoot. He in turn is assisted by the second assistant director and third assistant director. These last are essentially the stage managers and, on a film shoot, are responsible for props, actors, transport, etc. The third assistant is also sometimes referred to as a runner acting as a general 'gofer' as well as (usually) seeing to the transport of the actors.

In **BBC television** the stage manager is referred to as the assistant floor manager or AFM, working to the production manager, the areas of responsibility being broadly the same — props, actors and transport. The third assistant is then referred to as second AFM or floor assistant.

In the studio the production manager is also the floor manager, as he or she is responsible for what happens on the studio floor and the stage manager is the assistant — which is how the title AFM appeared.

In **Independent television** the AFM is referred to as the stage manager. Again it is more or less the same job, but with a different title. Television being a fluid industry and always changing, the job titles tend to change too so there are many grey areas; but the job of television stage manager, whatever its current title, concerns the areas covered here which, broadly speaking, are six in number:

- Pre-production.

- Rehearsals.

- Props.

- Actors.

- Liaison (in very many forms).

- Post production (at the time of writing this does not apply to the BBC).

Chapter One

PRE-PRODUCTION

This period can vary from a few days to a few weeks, depending on the size of the project and its budget and is the period before the filming actually starts.

Use the time to read and 'break down' the scripts. Read them through so that you know the story and are familiar with the characters.

'Breaking down' the scripts means marshalling the scenes into specific groups that make it easier for you to organise things — for example, grouping scenes that occur in one location together, so that when you go to film in that location you will know which props you need to take there.

There may be a list attached to the front of the script of some of the people working on the production — producer, director, costume, make-up, etc. There may also be an outline of the timetable — date of rehearsals, date and location of filming and so on.

Try to meet, or certainly 'phone, all key personnel on the project and see that they have received scripts and have read them as well. Establish your liaison process with every individual, particularly the director and the designer, so that you can consult them about their requirements and talk to the production manager about the areas he wants you to start working on. For example, some may leave transport entirely to you, others may want to be more personally involved, etc.

The production team

The immediate team will usually consist of some or all of the following:

Director
Production manager
Location manager
Assistant floor manager/stage manager
Production assistant.

There may be more than one of these teams working to a producer, whose own immediate team consists of:

Producer
Associate producer
Script editor

Producer:
The person in charge of the project. In the BBC they will be responsible to the head of the department.

Production associate
In charge of the financial and logistical side of things. Also advises on locations and facilities that may be required and if there is more than one production team involved in a project maintains liaison between them.

Script editor
Responsible for the script being in accordance with the producer's brief, of a suitable standard and usable. Liaises between the producer and the writers. Once the script is accepted the script editor is the writer's representative on the production.

Director:
The director is responsible for the artistic realisation

of the script and is the AFM/stage manager's immediate team leader.

Production manager/first assistant
The senior member of the director's immediate
team and the PM controls the organisation of the
actual process of putting the show together from
preparation through to recording. The PM is also
responsible for budgetary control and safety.

Assistant floor manager/stage manager
The AFM works to the director and PM and is responsible for ordering action properties (props) for rehearsal, filming, OB and studio and keeping them
safe. Close liaison with the designer is important
here. The AFM 'marks up' the rehearsal room floor
with the different sets required to rehearse in and
also keeps the script up to date, noting down artists'
moves and any dialogue changes. (The script is also
known as 'the book'). The AFM is also responsible
for prompting during rehearsal, operating spot effects and providing assistance wherever else the
director or PM may require it.

Production assistant
The PA works to the director and is responsible for
the administrative work the production requires
and for continuity on the set, i.e. that artist, prop and
costume details in different shots match each other
properly. In the prop area this is a job often shared
with stage management. The PA will also be the
director's immediate assistant in the studio control
room or 'gallery'.

Costing

In the BBC the production associate prepares a
departmental budget estimate outlining the
money, staff and resources that the production will

9

require. He will then tell each department within the production how much they can spend.

Make sure your other possible requirements — transport, armourers, etc all fall within the budget. Ask for quotes for things that might be expensive — don't just order them automatically because they have been asked for. Work closely with the design buyer and production manager and keep them informed.

Transport

This area falls under stage managements' responsibility. In the BBC unit cars for use by the production team and mini buses and coaches for recce-ing locations and ferrying artists and supporting artists about during shoots are arranged through transport department. You will also need a props van/lorry to keep your props in, if you are going away to film. Make sure you order one that is the right size!

Planning meeting

During the preparation period there will be meetings with Design, Costume and Makeup so that any 'grey areas' can be talked through — is a certain item going to be supplied by Props or Costume?— for example. Wallets and bags often fall into this grey area, more of which later. Clothes and accessories not actually worn are usually supplied by Scenic Operations Facilities in the BBC.

The usual accessories supplied by Costume and Makeup are parasols and umbrellas, watches, rings and jewellry that is to be worn, complicated badges that are a part of an actor's makeup, and spectacles.

Strand/Series Title	THE BRITTAS EMPIRE (D) p. 7				**VISUAL EFFECTS REQUIREMENTS**			
Programme Title					Distribution		Denotes Recipient	No of Cop
Episode/ Sub. Title					To:-		Room No. and Building	
Costing Number		Prod. Costing Wk(s)		Channel	Visual Effects Org.	GO7 250 Western Avenue		2
Programme Identificat'n Number			Studio		Studio Management Assistants (Co-Ord)	4044, T.C.		1
Production date(s)			Week(s)		T.S.O.	C307 Centre House		1
Filming/O.B. date(s)			Week(s)					
					Room No. / Building	Tel. Extn.	Department	
Producer							File Copy	1
Director							Date	*
Designer								
Rehearsal Room Phone No.		Film Location					Date Rec'd	

PLEASE ATTACH MARKED-UP SCRIPT			VISUAL EFFECTS USE ONLY	
DATE REQD. IF KNOWN	ITEM	DESCRIPTION – PLEASE STATE WHETHER REQUIR•D FOR STUDIO OR LOCATION	EFFORT HOURS	MATERIAL £
		Sc 14 – STAFF TOILET		
		32. Blackish slimy gunge – from waste pipe		
		EPISODE 6 – SAT 30 OCT. TC6		
		Sc 10 – BOILER ROOM		
		33. Dummy B/W kitten – to match real kitten Also seen in STUDIO.		
		34. Dummy kitten blown out of flue pipe by compressed air at 80 mph		
		Sc 17 – BOILER ROOM		
		35. Furnace in Boiler room		
		36. Artists reignite boiler		
		EPISODE 8 – SAT 13 NOV. TC6.		
		Sc 6 & 19 – STAFF ROOM		
		37. Clock – constructed to look like a (19th forge. Under the clock face – a furnace, an anvil & a blacksmith holding a hammer. Blacksmiths arm to rachet upwards & bang down sending out a shower of sparks.		
		Signature	HOURS	£
			£	£
			(FO8)	(137)

(i)   A Contract form will be provided as soon as possible; non-return of the form within four working days will be taken as acceptance of the Charge.
(ii) Where time allowed for completion of the work does not permit this procedure the Charge may be agreed by telephone and confirmed by a Contract form.
(iii) Please number each item separately.

Technical planning meeting

There will also be a technical planning meeting with the lighting director, the technical co-ordinator, sound supervisor and designer. The production operative supervisor should come as well. From meetings with the designer and director you will get details of the sets and furniture — the size and type of different pieces and their positions within the sets (see pp.16/17). Also now is the time to sort out things like lighting and fires — if electric the electricians provide them, but will there be oil lamps and candles? If so, you will have to provide them (don't forget to pack the matches!). Also there may be water in the studio. Any kind of flame or water constitutes a hazard and, in the BBC, has to be mentioned on the hazard form (see p.41).

Also check if there are any special requirements like working 'phones and intercoms and liaise with the sound supervisor and buyer accordingly to make sure they are practical (that is that they work) and that they will be properly wired up. Also note things like special effects (rain on windows, etc), which way cupboard doors will open, what kind of lock a door may have — things which are not your responsibility, but which could be vital during rehearsals.

The time of the technical run may also be fixed at the planning meeting — this is a run of the show for the technicians so that they can make their lighting and sound plans for the studio.

Read through your script again and make your prop lists, for both rehearsal and the real thing, lists of effects to inform the Visual Effects department (see p.11) about any graphics you may need, etc. It is advisable to attend to all these things as soon as possible because you may not have time later.

Chapter Two

REHEARSALS

If a show is to be shot in a studio, it is customary to rehearse it not only for the actors' sake, but also so that the director can decide where to put the cameras. As studios are expensive, rehearsals are usually conducted somewhere else. This means that a quick reproduction of the studio set needs to be made to rehearse in. This is done by taking the plan of the set, produced by the designer and from it marking the plan down on the rehearsal room floor with special marking tape. The scale used on the plan is usually one to fifty.

Assuming a dark coloured floor, the best coloured tape to use is yellow or white so it can be easily seen. Often there will be more than one set involved and the rehearsal room will be comparatively small, so it will be necessary to lay different set tapes one on top of the other. Use a different colour tape for each set and work out the positions by copying the different plans on to tracing paper and laying them on top of each other until the clearest combination is discovered. (The usual way to indicate ceiling pieces, arches or anything else that is fixed overhead is with a broken line and you'll find it easier to remove it if you lay it on top of a solid line the same colour as the floor.)

Then transfer this on to the rehearsal room floor. If you are unhappy about copying it straight down in tape use chalk first to plot out the lines and lay the tape along those. Then position the items of rehearsal furniture, trying to get the floor space taken up by them as close to that taken up by the real

thing as possible. Actors will always walk through tape 'walls' in rehearsal and then seem surprised when there is flattage (scenery) there in the studio!

Try to put background (dressing) furniture against the walls — anything will do!

Always try to leave the director some space in front of the set so that there is plenty of room for manoeuvre. It is also usually best to position a set so that the 'fourth wall' (the audience standpoint) faces the nearest window, i.e. the director's back is to the window when he is facing the action. Otherwise the director will be squinting into the light. Sometimes the director will tell you the way he wants the mark-up laid out.

It is always a good idea to provide some extra chairs so that the actors have somewhere to sit when they are not involved in the rehearsal and a large, im-mobile extra table so that the director and actors can sit round it when they have an initial read-through of the script. If you also provide coffee, newspapers, etc in this area it will stop the artists from wandering away when you want them.

Models

The designer may have made a model of the set and this is extremely useful to have in rehearsal, providing an invaluable check for ceiling pieces, rostra, stairs, etc and for the lighting and sound departments to look at when deciding where to position lights, booms and so on. Directors and actors find them handy too!

Also keep a look out for 'swingers' — a hinged flat that can swing back to allow access to a camera, 'traps' — hinged doors above floor level which can swing back to allow a camera access and 'floaters' — independently standing flats that can be wheeled in and out of position. Make sure these are marked on your floor plan.

Some reminders:

- Make sure you have the correct scale (BBC ground plans are drawn to a scale of 1:50 — see p.16/17). The grids marked on the BBC studio and rehearsal room (at North Acton) floors are 600mm (i.e. 0.6 metres or 2 feet square).

- Remember to include all the windows on the plan (usually depicted as a double line) — important light sources.

- Try not to overlap sets, but if you have to due to lack of space, try to avoid overlapping sets with another that will be used directly afterwards in the running order and try to keep furniture moves to a minimum.

- If you are working on a series or serial where sets are used frequently, always put the 'stock' sets, which will be used in every episode, down first,

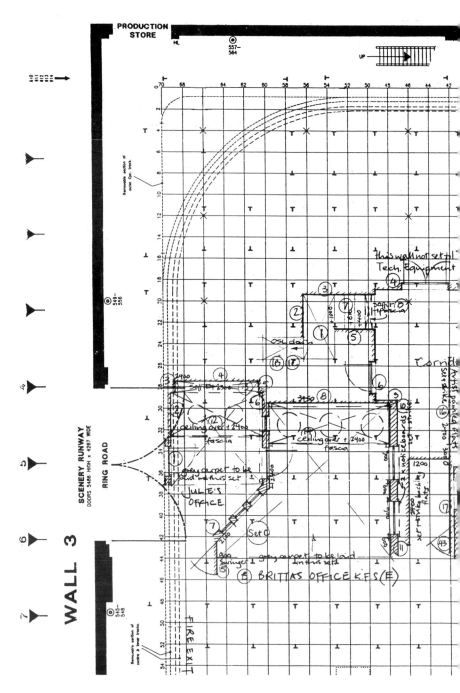

WALL 3

16

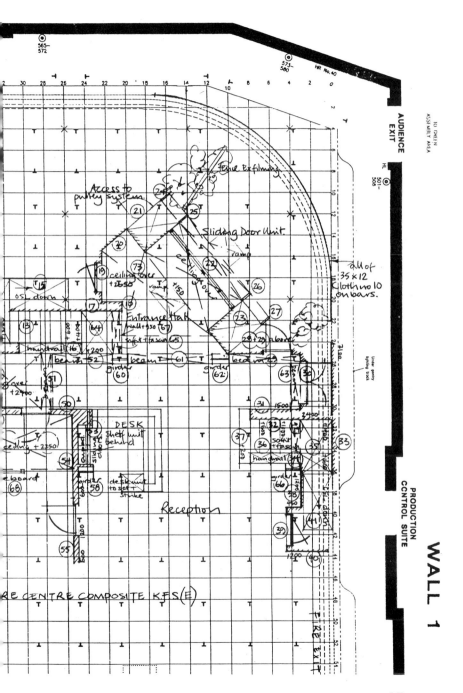

RE CENTRE COMPOSITE KFS (E)

then the 'keep sets', which are used more than once. Then the 'once only' sets go on top.

- Indicate which way the doors open with a tape arrow on the floor.

- Remember to include marker poles, if available, on the edge of each set so that the director knows if she is shooting off and to mark the edges of doors and entrances so that the actors don't 'walk' through walls when they enter a room.

- Try to match the rehearsal furniture as closely as possible to the furniture used in the actual set. If they are smaller, a director may find a carefully planned manoeuvre won't work in the studio because the larger furniture gets in the way. Liaise with the designer over this. The size and position of furniture is very important.

- The same applies to props. If possible try to get something as close to the real transmission prop as you can for the rehearsal — little details can make a big difference. But don't use the real thing. They could get lost or damaged and hire charges are expensive.

- Time is money. A good supply of tea and coffee on your large table stops the cast from wandering and stops you from being asked to go and fetch them and consequently missing vital moments of rehearsal!

Rehearsal schedule

These take a variety of forms and are affected by various factors — availability of actors (the rehearsal period is also used for costume fittings, makeup

consultations, publicity shots, etc) being obviously the strongest.

Sometimes directors are particular about the order in which they want to rehearse, the amount of time to devote to each scene and the number of times they want to rehearse each scene. Sometimes they have no specific demands.

Preparing the script

To make it easier to find your way around the script, tag the start of each scene and mark it on the tag. Mark the end of the final scene in each set and at the end of each scene mark the page number of the next scene in that set. It is a good idea to note the props required and any setting information at the head of each scene. (Always keep an eye out for details such as whether doors are open or closed, curtains drawn, the time of day — will lights be on and where is the light switch? — etc.)

19

Programme	THE BRITTAS EMPIRE (D)	OUTSIDE REHEARSAL REQUIREMENTS			
		Distribution	Denotes Recipient		No of Cop
Episode or Sub. Title		To:-	Room No. and Building	✓	
		Supervisor, O/R Unit	Victoria Road, N. Acton		2
Programme Number	50/LLC E448W	O/R Unit	Elstree		2
Studio date(s)	SAT 25th SEPTEMBER 1993	A.F.M.		*	1
Film date(s)		File Copy			1

Department	COMEDY	Room/Building	Extension	Date	*
Producer					
Director					
Designer					

O/R Room Address		Acton Room No.	Tel. No.	
Date Req'd at O/R	From: SAT 18/9/93 To: FRI 12/11/93	503		

CONTINUED   PAGE 2

REHEARSAL PROPS

23. 4 x desk phones
24. 1 x intercom
25. 4 x desk trays
26. 2 x briefcases
27. 2 x sports bags
28. 1 x bicycle
29. 1 x bicycle combination lock
30. 1 x drinking tankard
31. Pair os scissors
32. Large book
33. Rent book
34. Dogs travel box
35. Money till
36. Large drawer (detatched from a desk)- Deep
37. Hanky
38. Paper shredder
39. Assorted files - both box & cardboard types
40. Pair of sunglasses
41. Lengths of chain & padlocks
42. Camera
43. Bunch of flowers
44. Leaflets
45. Bell box
46. 6 x mugs

MANY THANKS   BECCY FAWCETT AFM ext 61808

'JULIET BRAVO' REHEARSAL SCHEDULE - page 2

MONDAY 17th OCTOBER   (Block the following scenes)

10.00	Scs. 2a,3,5,14,16,20, 22,27,34,36,47	Kate, Holden
11.30	Scs. 4,8,15,17,18,19, 24,25,26,28,29	Malcolm, Audrey
11.45	Scs. 30,31,32,33	Parrish, Audrey
12.00	Scs. 37,38 Scs. 40, 43,44	Parrish, Kate, Audrey Kate, Audrey
14.30	Costume fitting (TVC) for Audrey.	

TUESDAY 18th OCTOBER   (Work the following scenes)

10.00	Sc. 21	Beck, Parrish, Naylor
10.00	Sc. 46	Malcolm, Naylor, Beck
10.40	Sc. 45	Sparks, Parrish, Kelleher
10.45	Sc. 23	Kate, Parrish, Kelleher
11.00	Scs. 9 - 13	Kate, Sparks
11.10	Scs. 1 & 2	Kate, Naylor, Beck
11.15	Sc.6	Kate, Malcolm
11.30	Sc. 35	Kate, Beck
11.35	Sc. 41	Beck, Malcolm
11.45	Scs. 17 - 19,24 - 26,28,29	Audrey, Malcolm
12.00	RECAP ALL AUDREY SCENES	
12.30	RECAP ALL HOLDEN/KATE SCENES	

WEDNESDAY 19th OCTOBER   (N.B. No 'Malcolm')

Stagger through all possible scenes.

10.00		Kate, Holden
10.45		Audrey
11.15		Parrish
11.30		Beck, Naylor
12.00		Full available cast

Count how many pages a scene has and work out how much time to allocate to each one accordingly in the available time. If none of the above affects things, then you can fit in with actors' outside arrangements — opening of supermarkets, etc. Scenes may be rehearsed by set (so that the director does not have to trek back and forth between sets, especially if not all of them are marked up in the same room) or by a group of actors, so that they are not unoccupied for long periods until they are called on to rehearse again.

A schedule may look something like the example on p.21. Note that rehearsals are not necessarily in story order and that when a new character appears he or she is underlined. Try to keep to the story order whenever possible, though.

Rehearsals fall broadly into four sections:

Read through
The cast assemble for the first read through of the play. Check them off as they arrive and if anybody is decidedly late 'phone them to make sure they are on their way and that everything is all right. When all are assembled, inform the director and the read through will start. Afterwards there will probably be a break while the director and producer discuss things — you can liaise with Costume and Makeup at this point to make sure their fittings fit in with the rehearsal schedule.

Blocking
The first step of rehearsal is called 'blocking', where the director and actors decide what the essential moves will be — where an actor will stand up, sit down, walk to the door, take off his coat, etc. They may try out several moves before deciding which one is right.

Note the moves down very carefully because they are vital for working out the camera positions. Try and make your notes easy to decipher because the director may want to borrow your 'book' after rehearsals to check what the moves are. If furniture is moved during a scene, mark the original position on the floor in tape so that you can find it again.

General rehearsals

This is when the director and actors start 'working' the scenes — putting the art in. Interpretation of the script develops and camera angles are explored. The artists start to 'come off the book' (remember their lines without having to refer to the script) and the scenes start to come to life. This is where good prompting is required.

Runs

This is when the director rehearses the scenes in order to see how the story fits together.

Technical and producer's runs

At the end of the rehearsal period the technical run is taken in recording order (the order it will be recorded in in the studio) for all the technical people involved in the recording. (Remember for certain productions — game shows, for example — things like moving contestants, moving scenery and spot effects must be included). The producer's run is taken in story order, so that the producer can decide if it is all working as a piece of drama/comedy/whatever it might be.

The rehearsal begins

When running rehearsals, try to make sure that as many people as possible have a copy of your schedule. Don't forget people not immediately obvious, (i.e. in your office), as well as Costume, Makeup, Transport, for example.

In the rehearsal room make it very clear to everybody which scene is about to be rehearsed. Give episode, scene and set in a clear voice. *You are in charge.* Don't be afraid to call for quiet if necessary. When running a rehearsal scene you are responsible for:

- Setting props.

- Prompting.

- Marking down the movements in your script.

- Timing and word changes.

- Making notes for *anyone* not in the room at the time — Design, Costume, Visual Effects, etc. The production manager may not be present either, so remember to take any appropriate notes for them as well.

Positioning props

Note in your script ('book') where the actors and director want the props set and set them up accordingly the next time you run the scene. Remember to mark the position of furniture with tape on the floor and on the set plan in the 'book'. Remember to keep an eye on the positions of doors, curtains, etc. Remember little details such as the time of day the clocks should be showing. Keep a note of any prop setting/re-setting at the head of each scene. Keep the notes up to date as the positions often change during rehearsal and obviously keep your notes with you for when the scene is played in the studio!

You will also find that props not mentioned in the script may be required as a consequence of rehearsing the scene, so keep a note of them so that you can order them. The props list you made before you came to rehearsal may be markedly different from the one you find yourself with afterwards.

Prompting ('being on the book')

This is an art. There is nothing worse for an actor than to be in the middle of a meaningful and dramatic pause than to be suddenly 'prompted' by someone. Actors will sometimes say 'yes' or 'line' or something less printable when they 'dry' (forget their lines) and then you know you can come in — pronto! Otherwise, try and gauge when you think an actor needs helping out. Having made the decision, prompt clearly and distinctly — a mumbled prompt only leads to more confusion.

Don't be afraid to intervene if the actors 'jump' (miss out large chunks of dialogue) or alter a move

MARKED UP SCRIPT - Written Notation

6. INT. ROOM BEHIND DISCO. NIGHT

(A SMALL, SCRUFFY
ROOM WITH A KETTLE AND
INSTANT COFFEE. A SMALL
DESK AND TELEPHONE.

SOMETHING APPROXIMATING
TO AN OFFICE IN FACT.

MALCOLM LEADS THE WAY
IN, KATE BEHIND HIM.

THE DISCO MUSIC STILL
AUDIBLE)

① M+K IN DOORWAY (AS PLAN OPP.)

② M SWITCHES ON LIGHT

MALCOLM: ① So who's complaining
now then? ②

③ K+ C/R TO STAND BEHIND C/L CHAIR

KATE: I'm afraid I can't tell
you that. ③

④ M→ D/S OF DESK TO C/R CHAIR
FACES C/L

MALCOLM: (GRINNING)④ I'm not
going to send the heavy mob in,
don't worry. I'm not going to
break their windows or anything.
I'd just like to know, so maybe
we could sort something out - in
a civilised manner.

⑤ K SITS IN C/L CHAIR

KATE: I'll do any sorting out
that's needed, Mr Page. ⑤

⑥ M SITS IN C/R CHAIR

MALCOLM: Of course you will.
⑥
(contd....)

MARKED UP SCRIPT - Diagram Notation

6. INT. ROOM BEHIND DISCO. NIGHT.

(A SMALL, SCRUFFY
ROOM WITH A KETTLE AND
INSTANT COFFEE. A SMALL
DESK AND TELEPHONE.

SOMETHING APPROXIMATING
TO AN OFFICE IN FACT.

MALCOLM LEADS THE WAY
IN, KATE BEHIND HIM.

THE DISCO MUSIC STILL
AUDIBLE)

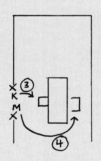

MALCOLM: ① So who's complaining
now then? ②

KATE: I'm afraid I can't tell
you that. ③

MALCOLM: (GRINNING) ④ I'm not
going to send the heavy mob in,
don't worry. I'm not going to
break their windows or anything.
I'd just like to know, so maybe
we could sort something out - in
a civilised manner.

KATE: I'll do any sorting out
that's needed, Mr Page. ⑤ ↓

MALCOLM: Of course you will.
                        ⑥ ↓
                (Contd ....)

that has been carefully 'blocked'. It is a good idea to keep your eyes on the actors as much as possible and only refer occasionally to the script. One way of keeping your place while doing this is to hold a pencil against the script and move it down the page at the pace at which the scene is moving, while watching the actors. The pencil will indicate the line you might need if an actor 'dries'.

Marking the movements

This varies in method from person to person. Obviously always use pencil as moves will change throughout rehearsal. Useful shorthand is: A.S. (as script), X (crosses) and OTM (on the move). Some people use a number system with a plan of the set opposite each page so that (1) in the script next to a line would correspond with a (1) marked on the set plan to show that the character said that line while in that position. Others use numbered short-hand instructions, arrows written next to the lines or even long-hand instructions. In the end you will have to choose whatever system suits you best.

Remember that in theatre moves are described from the *actor's* point of view, i.e. to move 'stage left' means to move to the right of the stage from the audience's viewpoint. In television and film, moves are from the camera's point of view — so 'camera left' means exactly that — left from the camera's viewpoint.

Always note any script changes and timings that come out of rehearsal and report them to the script editor (if there is one), the PA and the producer if he wants them.

Again, with your liaison hat on, report any changes arising from the rehearsal to the appropriate department. For example, the director may decide he wants the fire lit in the scene or a script change may call for it. Visual Effects will need to be informed as they will be responsible for the fire on set. Perhaps some action near the door is needed — an actor will take off a hat. Wardrobe needs to be informed that the character now wears a hat and design may want to provide a hatstand or hook, etc.

People who may need to be informed of things arising from rehearsal might be:

- Design
- Costume
- Makeup
- Visual effects (also known as special effects)
- Graphics
- Still photography
- Sound
- The buyer
- Production manager
- Production associate (BBC)
- Music
- Negative checks
- Transport
- Script editor
- Production assistant.

Other duties you may need to perform during rehearsals are:

- Answering the 'phone.
- Ensuring there is a reliable source of coffee.

- Spot effects (door bells, etc. A device called a bell-box is available for this purpose).

- Operating a tape recorder if one is needed.

- Making sure artists turn up for rehearsal, releasing them when they have finished and making sure they know their calls.

- Standing in for any 'supporting artists' who are usually only booked for the day of recording.

- Trying to keep the rehearsals to schedule by letting the director know if he is getting behind (tact required here!).

- Remember to clear up the rehearsal room when you leave and to tear your tape up off the floor.

Checklist for rehearsals

- Scripts (have several spare).

- Pencils (for you and anyone who hasn't brought one — i.e. most people).

- Erasers.

- Spare marking up tape.

- Stopwatch.

- Rehearsal props and furniture.

- Spare schedules.

- Chalk.

- Tea, coffee and biscuits.

- 'Phone, mobile 'phone, 'phone card.

- Tape measure

Chapter Three

PROPS

Action props (short for properties) are usually speci-fied in the script and are the equipment used during the dramatic action by an actor — as opposed to props that simply add to the ambience of the scene, which are known as dressing props.

Suppose we have a scene in which a robber wear-ing a mask drives a car up to a bank. He takes out a gun and a bag, goes into the bank, robs it and then as he runs out, his mask is yanked off in the process.

Immediately obvious props would be:

- The robber's car.
- The robber's bag.
- The money (see p.44).
- The gun (see p.43).

Less obvious, but equally important props for the scene would be:

- Other cars in the street at the time the robbery was committed.

- Handbags, walking sticks, shopping bags, dogs on leads, etc for passers-by in the street (see grey areas below).

- Handbags, briefcases, newspapers, etc for customers inside the bank at the time of the robbery.

- Papers and desk furniture for the tellers in the bank (see grey areas).

- Newspapers, pamphlets, etc that might be found lying around the interior of a bank.

- Anything else you can think of to dress up the scene.

The interior scene may be shot on location, in which case some of the above might be already there or in a studio where all of it would have to be provided but, in both situations, stage management would be responsible.

There are a couple of examples of 'grey areas' above. The robber's mask is pulled off, so that it becomes very much part of the action. But it will be provided by Wardrobe, as it is worn. Contact Wardrobe and make sure that the mask is easy to pull off and won't cause problems during the shoot.

Most of the papers on the desks, the 'phones, etc (what is known as the *dressing* — see above) will be provided by the designer.

However, if the action calls for someone to pick up a 'phone, stage management would ensure the 'phone is positioned where the actor can reach it.

'Prop' items and 'dressing' items often overlap, so it is a good idea to provide the designer with your prop list, or talk to him to find out what he is providing, so that the same things aren't acquired twice. DWS on your prop list means 'designer will select'.

Grey areas are a minefield. When in doubt, check.

When you first receive your script go through it carefully, noting down all the props that are actually mentioned and write these on the script at the head of each scene or maybe highlight them. Then note them down on your props list.

Be careful to spot and note any continuity props — that is props which appear in one scene and are also seen in a future one — and their appearance in another scene may be *implied*, not specified.

Don't forget that you may be filming the first scene on one day of a shoot and the next scene maybe weeks (or even months!) later and that the same continuity prop would have to be seen in both. Also continuity props can run between a location and the studio. You will have to look after that prop, or know where it is, for that intervening period. Always take a photograph. A small lockable box for valuable continuity props which you can keep with you is a good investment.

Some actors will also have a personal prop that they are never seen without, but that is never

BBC tv Property&Drape Requirements

Project No. 50/LLC E441L	
Ealing.	

File	Paper Colour

From Director MIKE STEPHENS

Room No. 4109 TC   **Extn.** 61808

To Manager Scenic Properties Buyers

Location/Country

Studio TC6

Copies to ____

Director (3) ____	Night Manager (Scenic Servicing) ____
Designer ____	Scenery Manager ____	Hired/Movement (2) ____

Production	THE BRITTAS EMPIRE (D)	**Filming O.B. Date**

Scenic Prop. Buyer	
Man. Props (O&S) (5) ____	**Memos to**
Petty Cash ____	T.O.M. ____

Designer JOHN BRISTOW	**Extn.** 67426	**Setting Date**

Booking Clerk ____	Catering ____
Designer Eal. ____	Sound Maintenance ____

Scenic Properties Buyer ALISON MACMILLAN	**Extn.** 61990	**Studio Reh.**

Film Op. Sup. Eal. ____	H/Engineers ____
Armourers ____	H/Electricians ____

Reh. Room No.	**V.T.R.**	**Data Due**

Order No.	H	T/C	**ZERO DELIVERY COLLECTION DATE**	**Data Recd.**

THE BRITTAS EMPIRE – STUDIO ACTION PROPS LIST

EPISODE ONE

Please can the following Studio action props be in TC6
by 08.30 a.m. on Saturday 25th September 1993.

SC 2 – STAFF REST ROOM

1. 10 x Pedal for a medal Achievement packs:
    10 x little plastic bags with "LIFE CYCLE WEEK"
        printed on one side – to contain:
    10 x badges that read "I pidelled for a medal"
    10 x signed certificates
    20 x coloured balloons
    10 x blood sugar urine testers
    10 x Leisure Centre logos
    N/B Continuity from filming

2. Engraved Glass Tankard Continuity from filming

3. 5 x assorted sports bags

SC 5 – RECEPTION

4. Mr Holroyd's bicycle – Continuity from filming

5. Combination bicycle lock – Continuity from filming

6. Pair of scissors – Continuity from filming

7. Large book – supposedly contains all the details of
    Whitbury Newtown Leisure Centre's special offers –
    See p.14

8. Rent book – WENDY

9. 10 x swimming tickets

PS/533 9.77.   **DO NOT TYPE BELOW THIS LINE**

referred to in the script, so also be aware of those — a filofax, or a special pen — something like that. If there is a choice of these, try to get actors to make their choice *before* you go into the studio. If possible, try to let them rehearse with them, too — but unless you have spares DON'T LOSE THEM!

Having noted the obvious props actually mentioned in the script, now think of less obvious ones. Don't forget that as well as the principal artists, all the supporting artists (extras) must be propped by stage management. If a scene is set in a hotel lobby, for example, provide newspapers, trays, coffee cups, bags, etc. Again, keep liaising — Costume *may* supply bags, spectacles are *always* provided by Costume because they are worn, etc. Talk to your director while you are drawing up your list so that you have as close as possible an idea of what she wants.

The action in a scene can be crucial too. Suppose we have a scene in which a wine bottle is opened and wine is poured out. If there were to be only one take you would need:

- Bottle of prop wine (obviously don't use real wine or artists' concentration may suffer!).

- Corkscrew.

- Glasses.

- Bucket (to dispose of used wine).

- Cloth.

However, scenes are rarely completed in only one take or set up. Your wine bottle has now been opened — you could hardly open it again, even if you could get all the wine back in — and everybody is getting impatient, ready for the next take. So, you order several bottles of prop wine. If the budget can stretch to it, eight would probably be a safe number. And tell the director that that is how many there are.

Let's take the scene a little further. The bottle has been opened and now the artists are drinking it. The scene is shot once and then again and again. This means that the bottle and glasses will have to be continually refilled as the 'wine' is drunk, and filled to the right levels for the 'continuity' in each shot to enable the different shots to be edited together in sequence. One of the artists breaks one of the matching glasses by accident. The glass is lost and wine goes everywhere. And so on.

The props list for the scene should look something like this:

1. Bottle of prop red wine x 8.

2. Two corkscrews (in case one breaks).

3. Matching glasses x 6 (4 artists and 2 to cover breakages).

OOV

4. Blackcurrant cordial or whatever prop wine is being used (to refill glasses).

5. Jug to fill them with.

6. Bucket to dispose of 'used' wine.

7. Funnel to refill bottle for continuity.

8. Cloths to wipe up mess when wine gets spilled.

Twice as many items as the previous list are required. The new items are OOV or 'out of vision' — i.e. they will not be seen on the screen, but they are just as important as the items that will be.

Your props list needs to be as specific as possible. Sometimes forms are provided for stage management to fill in and pass on to the buyer (if there is one), but detail is still important. Always try and talk through the list with your buyer as well. Something that is clear to you might not be to him or her and, if you're filming in the middle of Dartmoor or anywhere after the shops are shut, mistakes might be hard to rectify at a later date.

One of the most important areas is that of 'practicality'. If on your props list you were to write:

1. Mobile 'phone (F/P).

You would get a mobile 'phone that worked or was **fully practical** (F/P).

If you were simply to write:

1. Mobile 'phone.

You would get a dummy one — cheaper and less likely to break — a *dressing* prop. Not much use if you want a real one. So be specific and talk it through.

Be sure to find out where your props will be marshalled before the filming/studio and try to check them all with the buyer present if possible. You will already have made arrangements for them to get to location, usually in a van. Take very valuable items and those required first (as a precaution against the van breaking down) in your car.

Care of props is down to stage management or the props master (if there is one). It is a difficult area because no matter how many KEEP OFF signs you put on props, even when they are on the set, there is a strong temptation for them to 'walk'. Bowls of sweets or biscuits, for example, tend to have a short life span. Short of standing over them with a shotgun, which is usually impractical (and you'd need

an armourer!), there is little you can do. Always have more standing by. Plus more for re-takes! Valuable props should always be kept locked up and under the care of your prop man/prop master (if you have one).

Setting props

During rehearsal you will have noted on your script where the props are set or positioned at the beginning of each scene. When you come to the actual recording, if you are in a studio, it is best to set ahead as far as you can. Depending on the type of show the studio may have several sets in it at one time. Look at your recording order, which will have been prepared by the production manager, and set the props for the first scene in each set.

As soon as a scene has been shot in a set (and the scene has been pronounced 'clear' — that is, it has not been ruined by any technical problems), position the next collection of props required there, and so on. That way you will always be ahead of the game, which is a very good place to be. People don't mind waiting for cameras, lighting or sound, but they don't like waiting for Design or Props.

If scenes take more than one 'take' to get right, which they usually do, re-set the props as fast as possible. Your prop people, if you have them, will help with this. Give them a list of props for each scene before you start. Get one of them to work to you rather than setting/striking and remember them if they're good! This is one of the stage manager's most important professional relationships.

Drama recording tends to take longer than, say, situation comedies, and the propping varies accordingly. Sitcoms tend to move faster and maybe only go to two or three takes. Often they are done in one — speed of action keeps the audience on the boil. Sitcoms are also rehearsed in the studio more than dramas. Accordingly prop setting can almost be like that in the theatre — very fast.

On set, cupboards and sideboards make good hiding places for props, which can then be taken out and set — scenes are usually shot in story order. Conversely, drama scenes can go to over ten takes and need large reserves of props to cover them.

If there are large groups of complicated props involved in a scene, it is a good idea to take a polaroid of them at various stages of the scene's development, so that you can keep a track of them for continuity. The PA is also responsible for continuity and some productions have an actual continuity person, so you'll need to sort out who is responsible for what.

A polaroid is always useful — but obviously don't use the polaroid during a take! Also check with the camera operator that it is OK to use it as the flash affects some video cameras adversely.

Special props

Some props need special attention. The gun and the money and the dog on the lead mentioned in the bank robbery example at the beginning of this section are amongst them.

ANIMALS are usually regarded as props unless they perform some stunt or act in which case they are regarded as actors. They are usually provided by special agencies and come with a handler who will be responsible for them. In the BBC the authorities

PRODUCTION HAZARD ASSESSMENT (Continuation)

Details of activity and hazards identified:

WED 1 SEPT
1. Dog - booked by Artists Contracts. Has to perform various tricks in field. Using a performing dog.
2. Filming next to a swimming pool with swimmers in the water.

THUR 2 SEPT
3. Dog as above

FRI 3 SEPT
4. Children - to walk in a crocodile line in a corridor
5. 4 month old baby

SUN 5 SEPT
6. Artist to drive minibus in town centre
7. F/p guillotine. Artists head to be put on block

MON 6 SEPT
8. Liquid petroleum gas tanker to pull up at a garage

TUE 7 SEPT
9. Gas tanker - as above to pull up at Leisure centre
10. Camera on zip up tower
11. Artists on specially built single storey addition to rear of building

Precautions proposed, including details of experts engaged:

1. Booked with Handler Tineke Farr
2. Leisure centre lifeguards in attendance. Experienced swimmers
3. Handler as above
4. Children to come with chaperones
5. Baby to come with mother
6. Artist has full driving licence. Vehicle booked by Prop buyer through recognised supplier
7. Viz FX to operate. Blade never comes down when artist is near it.
8. Tanker to be empty. HGV driver to double as artist
9. As above
10. Tower supplied by a credited company
11. Constructed by scenic services

This form is issued by Television Safety Services who may be contacted for advice

Strand/Series Title	THE BRITTAS EMPIRE (D)				**BOOKING FOR ARMOURER**			
Programme Title					Distribution		Denotes Recipient	No of Cop
Episode/ Sub. Title					To: –		Room No. and Building	
Project Number	50/LLC E448W	Prod. Costing Wk(s)		Channel 1	Manager, Properties Operations and Storage		B1, Sc. Blk. T.C.	3
Programme Identificat'n Number			Studio					
Production date(s)			Week(s)					
Filming/O.B. date(s)	31/8/93 – 17/9/93		Week(s)					
					Room No. / Building	Tel. Extn.	Department	
Producer								File Copy 1
Director	MIKE STEPHENS				4109 TC	61808	COMEDY	Date
Designer	JOHN BRISTOW				4th F Sc B1	67426	DESIGN	25/8/93

IMPORTANT – A REQUEST TO TAKE FIREARMS AND WEAPONS ON LOCATION MUST BE MADE TO THE POLICE THROUGH THE CORPORATION'S INVESTIGATORS OFFICE ON EXTN. 4192 B.H. PLEASE STATE AUTHORISING POLICE OFFICER'S NAME, FULL STATION ADDRESS AND TELEPHONE NO.

Authorising Police Officer.............................. Station address.................................... Phone No ....
THE ABOVE DETAILS MUST BE COMPLETED BEFORE THIS BOOKING CAN BE ACCEPTED.

We require the presence of Brian Halliday for our filming
on Wednesday 8th September at:

Ringwood Recreation Centre
Parsonage Barn Lane
Ringwood
Hants

at 08.00am

The weapons we require are:

1. Assorted Roman spears & bows & arrows - for 10 x actors

2. 1 x High tech bow & arrow (rubber tipped) - not fired

None of the above are thrown, but are handled by the artists.

Many thanks

BECCY FAWCETT AFM   *Beccy Fawcett*

From : Manager Properties, Operations and Storage   Ext. 2451   Date

Subject : BOOKING FOR ARMOURER

To: Copy to Scenic Prop. Buyer

PROG. TITLE

VTR/FILM date(s)

THIS IS TO CONFIRM THAT .... HAS BEEN BOOKED AS ARMOURER TO SERVICE
THE ABOVEMENTIONED PRODUCTION.

(F.J. HOLLAND)

must be informed when an animal is coming into the studio.

Also, be aware of the Dangerous Wild Animals Act and regulations regarding the movement of livestock.

WEAPONS of any kind need to be accompanied, or their use sanctioned, by an armourer. If you are filming on location, even if you are using a toy gun, the police have to be informed (otherwise a well-meaning member of the public may see the action from a distance, think that a real shooting/murder is taking place and report it. If the police have been informed they will know what is going on).

Be aware of the differences between real/replica/dummy/toy weapons. A knife can be rendered less lethal by taping the blade in transparent

43

tape. ALWAYS talk to an armourer. Also in the BBC there is a Safety Department you can contact on any safety matter.

MONEY Certainly, where large sums are involved it is best to use dummy money. However, it is illegal exactly to reproduce UK currency. If you examine prop money carefully, you will find that there is always a slight defect from an exact copy, If you use real money always make sure you have some form of security for it. Be aware that it sometimes takes a long time to get hold of certain types of foreign currency.

FIRST AID AND SAFETY. Not really a prop, but you must always take a first-aid kit with you when filming on location (also consider getting first-aid trained — good for the C.V. and also for the injured!). You are also responsible for any special safety equipment that a particular location may demand — hard hats, for example, or life jackets.

For safety matters in general, national and company regulations can be complicated — if in doubt check with the Health and Safety Executive.

Chapter Four

ACTORS

Although the director directs the movements of the actors in the piece being filmed, it is the responsibility of stage management to get the actors physically from A to B and the places on the set that they are supposed to be in. Usually, in film, this is the realm of the third assistant director and in BBC TV the second AFM or the floor assistant.

Calls

To start at the beginning, once a rehearsal schedule has been drawn up, the actors are given their 'calls' — they are told where to be and when, usually over the 'phone! The PA (production assistant) will have prepared a cast list with addresses and telephone numbers of all the artists needed for rehearsal. It is usually best to call artists a couple of days before they are needed (even if you have given them a preliminary call some days before it is always advisable to give them a 'reminder' call closer to the time). Answerphones are a boon, but it is always a good idea to try to talk to artists personally, especially for their first call, in case there are any problems. Also, always remember to tell them WHERE they have to come to and, in the case of the BBC, check that their names have been left with Security so that they have no difficulty getting through the Main Gate.

A close record must be kept of the hours artists work and the scenes they appear in so that their overtime, if applicable, can be worked out. Time Sheets should be given to the PA. As rehearsals progress

Strand/Series Title	"THE BRITTAS EMPIRE" SERIES 'D'					**ARTISTS' STUDIO CALL SHEET**			
Programme Title	"NOT A GOOD DAY"					Distribution			Denotes Recipient
Episode/ Sub. Title	EPISODE 1					To:		Room No. and Building	✓
Costing Number		Prod. Costing Wk(s)	39	Channel	1	Beccy Fawcett		4109 TVC	*
Programme Identifcat'n Number	50/LLC E441D	Studio	TC						
Production date(s)	Sat 25 September, 1993	Week(s)	38						
Filming/O.B date(s)	29/8/93-17/9/83	Week(s)	35-37						

		Room No. / Building	Tel. Extn.	Department	
Producer					File Copy
Director	MIKE STEPHENS	4109 TVC	61808	L E (C)	Date
Designer	JOHN BRISTOW	4th Fl Des Bldg	67426	Design	00/00/93

ARTISTS	DATE: SATURDAY 25 SEPTEMBER				DATE:			
	Costume or Make-Up call	Studio call	RELEASE		Costume or Make-Up call	Studio call	RELEASE	
			Instruction	Action			Instruction	Action
CHRIS BARRIE	0000	1030	0000	21 CC				
JULIA ST JOHN	0000	1030	0000	"				
JUDY FLYNN	0000	1030	0000	''				
MICHAEL BURNS	0000	1030	0000	"				
HARRIET THORPE	0000	1100	0000	''				
PIPPA HAYWOOD	0000	1100	0000	"				
TIM MARIOTT	0000	1030	0000	''				
RUSSELL PORTER	0000	1030	0000	''				
JILL GREENACRE	0000	1030	0000	''				
ROSIE TIMPSON	0000	1100	0000	15·15				
COLIN SPAULL	0000	1130	0000	21 CC				
S/As								
CHARLOTTE BULLOCK	0000	1100	0000	15 15				
ANN BUCKLEY	0000	1100	0000	20 45				
JOHN CARRIGAN	0000	1030	0000	20 10				
CAROLINE LYNDSAY	0000	1030	0000	20·10				
MELANIE GRANT	0000	1030	0000	20 10				
MICHAEL LEADER	0000	1400	0000	21 CC				

the original schedule may change and actors, obviously, have to be kept abreast of this. Always give them a full rehearsal schedule).

Incidentally, always call actors by their real name, although their character name will appear on the schedules. It is unprofessional to call them by the name of the part they are playing.

If the recording takes place in a **studio** the actors need to be given their call times there as well. When recording, not only the time on set, but also the time required in Costume and Makeup beforehand, must be given to them — and these can be lengthy procedures, especially for a period show. At the end of each day's recording, if the schedule has had to be changed, the calls for the next day must be re-issued so that everybody knows. This is your job.

If the filming is on **location** the actors usually stay in the unit hotel with everyone else. Again, they must be kept up to date with their calls. One sure way to do this is to slip a piece of paper with their next day's call under their hotel room door so you can be (reasonably!) sure they have got it. Also make sure they know *where* to go for costume, makeup, the minibus or whatever. If in doubt always *over-estimate* the time.

To work out the call times you will need to know what that certain time is, how long it takes to drive there and how long each actor will need to spend in Costume and Makeup. These will sometimes operate at the hotel and sometimes in caravans at the location.

All the supporting artists will have to pass through Costume and Makeup too and this can sometimes take a while, especially if it is a period piece, for

MONDAY, 30TH MAY   LOCATION SHOOTING SCHEDULE

UNIT CALL: 15.30 to shoot

LOCATIONS: 4.   Rosehill Avenue   CONTACT: Mr & Mrs Smith
               Burnley

          5.   Bacup Police Station   CONTACT: Inspector R. Newton
               Bank Street   Tel.: Bacup 873350
               Bacup

DIRECTIONS FROM UNIT HOTEL TO LOCATION 4 (see Map C)
Walk out of Rosehill House Hotel driveway and the location is facing you.

DIRECTIONS FROM LOCATION 4 TO BASE (5) (Dinner rendezvous)
(Travelling time 15 minutes)   (see Maps D + E)

Turn right out of hotel into Rosehill Avenue, then turn left on to
Manchester Road. Go over the pedestrian lights. At next set of lights
turn left following signs to Halifax, Bacup and Todmorden. At T-junction
turn right sign-posted Rochdale A671 and Bacup. As you approach Bacup
you will see the Irwell pub on the left. Bacup Leisure Hall is just
beyond it on the right, set back from the road.

PARKING: LOCATION 4:   In the Rosehill House Hotel car park

             LOCATION 5:   At Bacup Leisure Hall and in the car park
                          outside the police station

COSTUME/MAKE-UP/TOILET – for Loc.4 at Rosehill House Hotel
PHONE FACILITIES

DINNER AND PHONE FACILITIES – for Loc.5 at Bacup Leisure Hall

ADDITIONAL TOILETS – At Bacup Police Station

SEQUENCES TO   EP.5 TK 1c p.3   Road outside Butler's House   DAY 1
   SHOOT   Colin Butler .... RICHARD KAY

            EP.5 TK.2 p.9   Ext. Butler's Lounge   DAY 1
               Colin Butler .... RICHARD KAY
               Josephine Butler .... MICHELLE BAGULEY

            EP7 beg. Scene 39 p.86   Ext. Butler House
                                NIGHT 2 (DAY FOR NIGHT)
               Ellen .... JAN CAREY
               Josephine .... MICHELLE BAGULEY

ARTISTS CALLS: EP.5 artists to be ready on Location 4 at 15.30
              EP.7 Artists to be ready on Location 5 at 21.00

TRANSPORT: Coach to leave Rosehill House Hotel on wrap at
              Location 4 (approx. 19.45) with artists and staff
              and travel to Bse (5) for dinner. Then to work as
              directed.

PROPS/DESIGN   2 Butler family cars – to be on Location 4 at 15.30.
VEHICLES   Design to dress Butler's house Int./ext. as required.
              Kate's Maestro and Duckworth's car to rendezvous
              with unit at Base (5) at 20.00.

CATERING: Tea on Location 4 at 16.30 for 35 people
              Dinner at Base (5) at 20.00 for 35 people
              Hot rolls at Base (5) on wrap (00.30 approx) for 35

TECHNICAL   As discussed at recce
REQUIREMENTS: Location 5 to be lit by 22.00

example. (Costume may ask you to request the supporting artists to wear their own clothes for the shoot when you call them).

All these different times have to be co-ordinated so that everybody is ready at the same time. Then they must be taken to the location. Methods of doing this differ, but there is usually a coach or minibus of some sort. If the locations are in a city, local taxi fleets can be used — open an account with one. And, of course, there will be unit cars as well — one of which will be driven by you.

On a typical morning's filming, there could be five principals and perhaps ten supporting artists to be at a location at a certain time — all of which must be supervised by the third assistant. Let the location manager know the first call if Costume and Makeup are on the location so that she knows what time to be there to oversee things.

Always explain everything. Never assume anything. A film set can be an emotionally charged place and when this is coupled to the 'holiday' type atmosphere that staying in a hotel away from home can produce, even when you are working very hard, it is important for stage management to try and remain calm, or at least look as if you are remaining calm. Aim to be the fount of all knowledge and remember to bring a loud alarm clock. Actors may look to you for support, maybe unconsciously, but encouraging words and close attention to their needs can work wonders and also make life easier for you.

It is also a good idea to try and pace yourself. A third assistant on a longish shoot will probably work longer hours than anyone else (maybe Design comes close). Be aware of this and try and organise yourself accordingly. Delegate where you can.

Chapter Five

LIAISON

This is the most important part of the job. Communication is the magic word in television and film production. Lack of it causes a lot of problems and lots of it oils the wheels better than anything else. Communication is one of stage management's chief functions, on many different levels.

- When drawing up your props list always liaise closely with Design and pass copies of your list to all interested parties as well as the buyer.

- Make sure the notes you make on your script are legible. Directors may want to check them for the moves and others may want to know the position of furniture, etc.

- Negative checking. This is to ensure that anything seen on the screen is either fictional and cannot be confused with anything in real life or is used with the owner's permission. For example, car number plates, 'phone numbers, road names, house names, names of people, shops and businesses, trade marks, etc.

  They can be checked in several ways — with Companies House, the Patent Office, the Mechanical Copyright Protection Society, the Performing Rights Society, Music, Video, Film and Still libraries and production companies' legal departments. There is some overlap here with the PA, script editor and producer, but be aware that it needs to be done.

- Once you are shooting, if there are any changes in the order make sure everyone, especially Costume and Makeup, knows.

- When on the set you may be required to shout for quiet for a take, or to use the red light and bell. When these are switched on all activity on the set should cease for the take.

- Stopping traffic is an important liaison job. Police are often employed for this on location, but they can't be everywhere and traffic control is often an area for stage management. Always be polite and if a driver becomes objectionable try and keep him or her talking. By the time you have finished with any luck the take will be over. (You may *not* force a driver or pedestrian to stop on a thoroughfare). Also, nobody on the production can be forced to stop traffic if they don't want to.

- Cueing could be looked on as liaison — you are communicating between director and actor. Always be clear and definite with a cue and obviously make sure that the actor can see it (or hear it). It is surprising how often this doesn't happen. Also, if you are giving a prompt, do not get in the artist's eyeline.

- If you are using walkie talkies on a location, be clear. Press the talk button well before you talk. Keep radio traffic precise and *never use bad language on air* — it is illegal.

In short, if you find out about or hear about something that somebody on the production ought to know, *tell them*. Don't assume someone else has.

Chapter Six

A TYPICAL SHOOTING DAY

The following outlines a typical shooting day from the stage management's point of view both on film and in the studio. Filming falls into two sections as it often utilises two AFM's — one for props and one for artists. If there is only one AFM they will obviously have to deal with both!

Film

Props

You will have compiled your basic props list well before filming starts and distributed it to the appropriate people (see Chapter Three). If you are away filming 'on the road' the props will be on the prop waggon and you liaise with the prop man about your daily requirements.

On the filming day make sure you have the details of where the filming location is. These are usually found on the schedule, together with maps.

The location manager deals with any problems/information directly connected with the location and is the person you go to with problems about parking prop vehicles, etc. You may already be familiar with the location if you went on the camera recce. (It is always helpful to go on these so that you can anticipate any problems that may arise at the location and talk them through with the appropriate people beforehand.)

Before filming give the list of prop requirements for the day to your prop man together with any necessary calls to large 'props' such as in-vision vehicles, so that they know where to turn up and when (don't forget to sort out the parking!). Always call them well before filming starts, so that firstly, they actually turn up on time and, secondly, if they are inherently mechanically unreliable — vintage cars, carriages and waggons, for example — you can make sure that they are actually working and mobile before the cameras start to roll.

N.B. A couple of points here:

- If you are working on a period piece with horses and carriages NEVER stand behind a horse.

- Always remember that it takes a much longer time and larger space to turn a horse and carriage round for a re-take than a car. First assistants may need reminding of this.

As soon as you arrive at the location (again, well before filming starts) check that you know where two very important things are — the lavatory and the catering waggon. People will ask you these questions all day. Having established this, find your prop man and check that all the props for the day are there and that you are set up for the first scene. From then on, together with the prop man make sure that throughout the day props are available in the right place at the right time. Don't wait to be asked for them! And keep an eye on continuity.

You also assist the PM/first assistant as necessary which might entail marking artists' and vehicles' positions (tape or chalk are usually used for this; however, if the ground is in shot try and use something that will blend in like a pebble or a twig), controlling traffic and crowds (it is sometimes a good idea to wear a luminous jacket), cueing artists and vehicles, trying to control noise (for example,

"Stopping traffic is an important liaison job ..."

politely asking pneumatic drill operators if they could please stop drilling for just five more minutes) and a thousand and one other things which a day's filming can entail.

At the end of the day make sure the prop man knows what is needed tomorrow and that the vehicles, handlers with their animals and other large 'props' know their calls, having checked them with the production manager. Then help the production operatives to clear up so that the location is left as you found it (remember to order a large quantity of black rubbish bags, brushes and shovels on your prop list. There are few things messier than a film unit).

Artists
The schedule should have a list of 'useful' numbers, such as that of the coach firm, as well as the artists' names and telephone numbers for easy reference.

Make sure everyone involved has a copy of the schedule as early as possible. The day before, work out the artists' and supporting artists' individual calls with the PM (even if it's only to be told 'as on the schedule — no change'), Costume and Makeup and give them accordingly. Also, keep artists who are due to join the unit in a few days' time broadly appraised of what is going on as schedules can change all the time.

On the day of filming check off the artists' and supporting artists' names on your list as they arrive. In the BBC, if they are called to Television Centre they will be issued with dressing rooms. On location, Costume and Makeup may install themselves in the hotel or in caravans at the location, or both. Depending where it is, see the artists and supporting artists through them and on to whatever mode of transport is being used — minibus, coach, taxi or unit car. Keep the appropriate 'phone numbers handy for when they don't turn up! Also check that any coach that arrives really is for you and not for someone else.

Remember that you may also need to transport Costume and Makeup staff and various others (armourers, for example), so make a list of everyone who needs transport and don't go off without them. Always, always make sure that the drivers know where they are going and have maps.

As soon as you arrive at the location, let the PM/first assistant know and find out how soon the first artists are required so that you can have them on the set when they are needed. It is essentially your job to know where all the artists are at all times, which is not easy. Try and familiarise yourself with the behaviour patterns of the more eccentric artists, so that if they do go AWOL you have a fair idea of where they might be.

You are also responsible for keeping a record of the hours the artists work (their 'call' and 'release' times) and the best way to do this is to complete a call sheet (see p.46) on which you record start and finish times, travel time, stand-by days, travel days, etc. Give this to the PA who, incidentally, will probably have a preference for the type of call sheet to use.

Supporting artists' hours can be kept in a similar but less detailed way — remember to make a note if a supporting artist is made up to a 'walk-on' by the PM (this means the supporting artists will be given more to do and thus be paid more money — check this with your PM). Childrens' hours are very strictly controlled and the PA often keeps a check on this.

You will also frequently be in charge of getting morning and afternoon coffee and tea to the location if the caterers are based some distance away — and occasionally guarding it when it arrives there.

Remember that you don't only have to get everyone to the location — you have to get them back again too!

The Studio

Props
In the studio everybody works from the camera script, which has the camera shots on it. Transfer the notes from your rehearsal script — props for each scene, furniture positions, etc — on to it.

A recording order, listing the scenes in order of shooting will also be issued and it is a good idea to mark props, etc needed on this for an at-a-glance reference. You can give one of these to your prop man.

The production manager liaises with the production operatives about scenery moves, but it is important that you are aware of them too.

Depending on circumstances, a show can be set in the studio during the day or overnight. If it's being set in the day you can go and see how the work is progressing and whether your action props have arrived. If they have you can try and identify them, which will save time on the day of recording. Whatever you do, don't put action props on the set yet — during setting a studio resembles the first day at the Harrods sale with furniture and fittings flying everywhere. Wait until the designer has finished, which usually means waiting until the recording day.

On the day of recording come in early and check that your action props are all present — they may be in the 'cages' that are used to store things safely or they may have been set out separately or the buyer may bring some personally, so it may take a while to track them all down. Spend some time with the buyer so that you know where everything should be. In the BBC some cages set aside for valuable items have special security locks that can only be opened by the production supervisor or the loss and damage department.

Set your props in the manner discussed in the earlier chapter. If you can arrange it, have a table or area exclusively for props where you can lay everything out and see at a glance what you have got. Otherwise it is very easy to drown in a sea of wrappings, boxes, buckets, etc. Remember that hired items often have a sticker on them which has to be removed and this can take some time. If you have food in a scene, order a hot trolley so that you can keep it warm and a fridge for cold items.

The day may begin with the director, who sits in the control room or gallery (though they do occasionally come out on to the 'floor' which is what the main body of the studio is called), blocking the scenes for the camera operators. He communicates with everyone on the 'floor' through the production manager, via two-way talkback.

You can get a set of 'cans' (talkback) from the floor assistant so that you can hear what is passing between the director and the production manager. Some AFM's prefer not to because they find it interferes with their concentration as they are usually occupied setting several sets ahead of the one being talked about. If you wear talkback, keep one 'can' on one ear, but the other ear free — that way you can hear what is going on around you as well.

When a scene is being played, stand by with your prop man to re-set props and furniture, marking positions where necessary. You can see the shot that will be used for the transmission, because that will be the one featured on the many monitors on the studio floor.

The production operatives are there to rig and operate scenic equipment and captions and certain effects such as smoke guns. They will set and strike scenery, furniture and props and will help you with the preparation and setting of food and the washing up afterwards. They will also mark positions of artists.

Often recording occurs in rehearse/record mode which means what it says — a scene will be rehearsed and then recorded immediately afterwards.

While setting ahead:

- Be aware, of any re-setting necessary in the set that is being recorded in so that you can deal with it at the appropriate moment.

- Never throw anything away, even after a scene has been recorded. It may have to be done again and those props will be needed back!

- Always wear soft-soled shoes in the studio so that you don't make a noise.

- Always keep out of the actors' eyelines.

When the recording is finished check that any continuity props (props needed in a further episode) are marked with a label and kept safe and that anything valuable is locked away.

Artists

Dealing with actors in the studio within the BBC is the job of the floor assistant. There are not quite as many problems involved as with filming because they are all coming to one place and there are fewer opportunities for them to wander off. Essentially the job is the same — to make sure they have arrived, get them through Costume and Makeup and on to the set at the right time. Stage management needs to check that any necessary cars/taxis have been organised and at the end of the day that any appropriate calls for the following day have been issued.

Chapter Seven

LIVE TELEVISION

So far, most of what we have discussed applies to recorded television. This section concerns live television.

This usually falls into the following categories:

- Music and arts.

- Childrens programmes.

- Light entertainment.

- Discussions.

- Events.

- 'Shows', e.g. Childrens' Royal Variety, BAFTAs.

- Sport.

- Live drama (extremely rare).

Your project may be in the form of live inserts into another live programme, e.g. *Going Live*.

Your live programme may well have pre-recorded inserts; there may be continuity implications, e.g. *Noel's House Party*.

Other programmes may be recorded 'As live', i.e. you are shooting a piece or event that is unrepeatable, even if it is not for synchronous transmission, e.g. a Royal Occasion.

Rehearsals

If you have outside rehearsals accurate timings are vital. Presentation (also confusingly known as Continuity) — the people who run the Network on which you will be transmitting — will need to know the duration of your programme and where the commercial breaks occur (these are run regionally on ITV and Channel 4) particularly if you are running up to an immovable event such as the news or a regional opt-out.

Studio rehearsals and transmission

You may find that a live show for which there is a predetermined script is rehearsed *ad nauseam*. You should really know what you are doing by transmission (TX)! However, directors being what they are, things do change at the last minute and will, as a consequence, be done unrehearsed.

Keep alert and listen to the talkback. As you should be happy by now with what you *thought* you were doing, you should be able to take on changes with a clear slate.

- Aim to have your prop operatives doing all the setting of props, etc — you will have worked this out in rehearsal. This leaves you free to trouble-shoot 'on the night' — particularly to assist the floor manager.

- If you have a problem that the floor manager needs to know about (i.e. it will affect the TX) try to have a solution for them. "The carafe has broken, I have replaced it with a jug" is better than "The carafe has broken, I don't know what to do!". Remember to speak very concisely and precisely, especially if the show is noisy — and quietly if it is not!

- The floor manager is under great pressure. Back him up. If he gives you an instruction or answer to a problem during the transmission do not question him unless absolutely necessary.

- It is very important to have the things and people for which you are responsible in place in plenty of time. Pay particular attention to briefing people about what they should be doing. Presenters/performers and members of the public alike can be very daunted by the prospect of working live and will probably make many more demands of you and your colleagues than usual. Be ready!

If you are only going to get your contributors just before transmission ensure the following:

- That you know *who* is going to organise their transport to and from the studio. It will probably be you. It will be widely assumed to be you if they do not turn up!

- To take the example of an M.P., be absolutely sure which part of the House of Commons your guest is expecting to be collected from, and when, and that you have told your transport office or department, who have told the cab firm, who have told the driver, who has written it down. It is worth paying the extra for a good car firm in these circumstances, preferably one where the drivers carry mobile 'phones. Get the numbers.

- If your contributor is in public life, they will probably need to go somewhere else after your programme — where and how?

- Make sure there is a system to inform the studio gallery/control room that a guest is running late. Give the gallery number to the guest, the car firm and the driver.

  While you are in the studio, there is unlikely to be anyone in the office and you will be unable to hear a 'phone on the studio floor as you will, by now, have taken it off the hook to stop it from disturbing the programme!

- If your guests' transport to the studio involves a rail or air journey, check who is issuing their tickets — it may again be you — and that the driver and guest know how to recognise each other at the airport/station. Know who to call for information about the time- keeping of the 'plane/train.

- Pay attention more than ever to the camera script and to where the equipment (especially large camera cranes) will move to during the show. The operators of this equipment expect those nearby to be aware of what they are going to do and when and they *must* get their shot. You may be doing something you had not re-hearsed— like getting a glass of water for some-body, and a sudden collision could result in an injured stage manager, a slippery floor and a thirsty guest.

There are three golden rules of live television:

1. At all times stay calm. It may be ten minutes to transmission, you don't have a running order, the presenter has disappeared and the most important guest is having a crisis in the lavatory. Announce cheerfully, while dealing with these upsets — "We're nearly ready — no problem!".

2. Never lose your sense of humour, though jokes tend to go down better with the crew than tense directors on talkback.

3. Always make sure you have plenty of cold, still (not fizzy) mineral water to hand.

Some potential problem areas

Ear pieces for the presenter rarely fit, even though they are often moulded for the wearer (they were fine in rehearsal!). Always have standard spares.

Guests/contributors sometimes arrive not knowing why they are there or what they are talking about (especially politicians) and there is no researcher or assistant producer around to look after them. Be ready to help them.

No-one told the *one* makeup artist that all the guests (arriving within ten minutes of each other and with ten minutes to go) were perhaps female

(requiring the full hair and makeup treatment), very light or dark skinned or allergic to all known brands of makeup.

Always check travel arrangements and arrival times with the assistant producer or researcher at least twice during the course of the day.

With bands and musicians remember that there will be more lorries, more roadies, more hangers-on than you ever thought possible (let alone were told about). Always call the set-up time and band call at least an hour earlier than the time you were given. (This allows for parking problems, people getting lost, forgetting the equipment, checking that their plugs fit your sockets, etc). N.B. This applies to pre-recorded music as well.

As ever, communication is the *essential* ingredient. Live television is fun but hard work — you have to be very organised. Having played your part in a hitch-free complex live programme is one of the most satisfying feelings in television. Afterwards!

Chapter Eight

FOREIGN FILMING

This is not a trouble free holiday, as some may think. It is usually a lot tougher than filming in the UK.

An early prop list is vital so that the buyer can find out what he can get locally. Some things can be flown out, others can't and everything needs Customs documents (carnets). Vehicles especially need plenty of notice and international driving licences for everyone may need to be sorted out, depending where you are. Details like graphics need early attention so that they don't have to be sent out to you — and check where the nearest photocopier is.

Armourers need a great deal of notice and detailed information about any weapons being used — these are obviously the sort of things to get seized by Customs unless the papers are exactly in order. Check everything with the armourers who are the experts here. Visual Effects also need detailed information about what they have to provide as, in the BBC, they deal with the shipping themselves. Details of safety equipment also need to be finalised early in the proceedings. Liaise closely with the production associate who will have made the initial contacts with authorities and suppliers — bookings will go through him.

Supplement the first aid kit with suitable additions — stomach upset pills, cures for sunburn, headaches, insect bites, etc and make sure you know where the local doctor is when you reach the location — choose one who speaks English, if possible!

Double check artists travel arrangements, documents, innoculations, etc and check local regulations for vehicles — height restrictions, movement restrictions, border Customs hours, etc. Try and find out as much about the country as possible, both from people who have filmed there to those who have just been there for a holiday. In foreign filming particularly, never take anything for granted.

When you get to the hotel make friends with the hotel manager whose local knowledge will be invaluable.

A few things to bear in mind:

- Remember which side of the road you should be driving on (including when you get back to the UK!).

- Have passport and papers with you at all times.

- Get the number of the British Consulate.

- Have a phrase book and try to learn vital phrases.

- Learn how the 'phones work.

- Remember that, broadly speaking, everything will take up to twice as long to do as it does in the UK for one reason or another.

- The cast will see you as a 'nanny' figure and expect you to know details of everything from how much a cup of coffee costs to the local train timeable. Try to be as prepared for these eventualities as possible.

Chapter Nine

POSTSCRIPT

In some independent companies it is stage management's job to make sure the right material goes to and comes from the edit. Obviously, it is very important to get this right or all of the above would have been for nothing.

Avoid travelling on underground trains with videotape — magnetic fields may damage it.

Make sure that airport security staff won't interfere with film or tape by checking with them *before* you travel.

You may be required to remain at an edit as a 'production presence'. It is useful to learn the editing process and jargon as you may well be asked by your production manager to ensure that time in such a very costly facility is being used properly. Learning the rudiments of editing will also help you appreciate the entire rehearsal and shooting process.

Post production and clearing up

In the BBC at the end of each project some time is allotted for 'clearing up'. This is when you complete your expenses forms and Time Sheets and return borrowed equipment like tape recorders, as well as CDs and books to the appropriate libraries.

If you are working on a series or serial make sure that the AFM who follows you knows what and where the continuity props are. The buyer will usually keep them safe.

A word about expenses. Sometimes they seem small and difficult to work out, but they can mount up and if you buy anything for the production AL-WAYS get a receipt and ALWAYS write what it is on the back so that when you are doing your expenses weeks later, you will remember what you had to buy.

Stage management in television is a very varied area and there are as many approaches to the job as there are people who do it. In the end, everything always comes back to communication — informing everyone who needs to know what is happening; being there when needed for the actors; supporting the PM and the director and, above all, remembering that successful TV is based on teamwork.

"Make sure the security staff don't tamper ..."

APPENDIX

It is useful for a stage manager to have certain things on him or her at all times. They are:

> Swiss army knife
> Pen
> Notebook
> Tape

It is also a good idea to have immediate access to some kind of toolbox with the following in it (no particular order):

> Tape measure
> Scissors
> Sash cord
> Fullers' Earth/talcum powder. (Don't use Fullers' Earth in the vicinity of studio cameras)
> Safety pins
> Pins
> String
> Elastic bands
> Water spray
> Cloths
> Bin bags
> Double-sided tape
> Chalk
> Cigarette lighter (and cigarettes for actors)
> Burnt cork (good for dirtying things down)
> Brown hairspray (ditto)

Washing-up liquid (stops hinges squeaking
— also for washing up)
Needle and cotton
Captions card — Double Crown — black on
one side and white on the other
Pencils
Eraser
Drawing pins
Blu-tak, black tak (a substance used by car
mechanics to fix windscreens to frames) and
white tak (stick 'n fix)
Camera card
Mobile 'phone
'Phone cards
Coins
Glue gun
Large black felt tip markers
Chamois leather
Staple gun/staples
Black felt (ten yards is enough!)
Polaroid camera and film
Biscuit tins
Hip flask
Maglite torch
Cork screw
Condoms (many uses!)
Fishing umbrella
Wet weather gear
Fishing line (varying strengths)
Padlock and key
Collapsible chairs
Stanley knife with spare blades
Petty cash float
Receipt book for above expenses.